Table of Contents

Introduction

The very existence of the North Atlantic Treaty Organization (NATO) during the Cold War was predicated on the need for common defense against the threat posed by the Soviet Union and Warsaw Pact. During the Cold War, the Alliance evolved into a political-military organization supported by an extensive and complex decision-making bureaucracy.[1] After the end of the Cold War, both the United States and the European members of the Alliance saw the utility in retaining this common defense system. However, over time their focus has required a geopolitical reorientation from within the sovereign boundaries of member nations to a concern with a broad range of security concerns. This transition has not come without debate and is not yet complete. The most intense element of the debate revolves around the geographic and strategic limits of NATO action. Since 1999, the Alliance, after a long history of out-of-area debates, has formally extended its security horizon beyond the geographic boundaries of its member nations, but it has yet to resolve how best to implement strategy to equitably ensure collective security.[2]

Though the rhetoric of the North Atlantic community has long enshrined the importance of democratic governance, the centrality of NATO as a collective security organization made up of democratically elected governments has been especially important in recent decades. With its expansion over the past two decades, NATO has emphasized the promotion of modern western

---

[1] For a detailed history of the institutional development of NATO and civil-military relations see Lawrence S. Kaplan, *NATO 1948: The Birth of the Transatlantic Alliance* (Lanham, Md.: Rowman & Littlefield Publishers, Inc., 2007); *The United States and NATO: The Formative Years* (Lexington, Ky.: Univ Pr of Kentucky, 1984). during the Cold War refer to Robert S. Jordan, *Political Leadership in NATO: A Study in Multinational Diplomacy* (Boulder, Colo.: Westview Press, 1979); and for a post-Cold War developments, see Ryan C. Hendrickson, *Diplomacy and War at NATO: The Secretary General and Military Action after the Cold War* (Columbia, Mo.: University of Missouri, 2006).

[2] Douglas Stuart and William T. Tow, *The Limits of Alliance: NATO Out-of-Area Problems since 1949* (Baltimore: The Johns Hopkins University Press, 1990), 319-22.

ideas about civil-military relations, namely civil supremacy over the military.[3] Generally, civil-military relations in alliances are more easily manageable and cooperative during times of peace. Under the pressure and uncertainty of war, when national survival itself may be at stake, the ability to compromise and develop clear strategy and obtainable objectives becomes exceedingly difficult.[4] This is further complicated in NATO as emphasis shifts from common defense, which seems a less likely mission, to out-of-area operations to improve the overall security environment. In the conduct of military operations outside of allied nations' sovereign boundaries, the spectrum of relations between Alliance forces and civilian authorities becomes more prohibitively complex and restrictive the farther these operations depart from alliance territory. It is the role of the military in the contemporary operating environment to advise on strategy formulation, propose options and explain risks to their civilian governments. The nature of this relationship will differ according to the type of activity being conducted and therefore different parameters apply along this spectrum of conflict. The approved strategy must be supportable and flexible, yet unambiguous enough to enable the establishment of concrete, attainable objectives.

Since the end of the Cold War, NATO has adopted two strategic concepts, first in 1991, then in 1999. A strategic concept provides the principle direction for the Alliance by identifying threats to security and outlining the fundamental approaches to combat those threats, especially

---

[3] For more information on the expansion of NATO see Anton A. Bebler, *The Challenge of NATO Enlargement* (Westport, Conn.: Praeger, 1999), additionally Gerald B. Solomon provides a study of the debate surrounding the expansion of NATO in the post-Cold War political landscape in *The NATO Enlargement Debate, 1990-1997: The Blessings of Liberty* (Westport, Conn.: Praeger, 1998).

[4] B. H. Liddell Hart, *Strategy* (New York: Signet, 1974), 353-54. Examples of this are numerous for both cases of limited war and existential war. In the case of limited war, like that in Afghanistan, collective strategic objectives are difficult to determine and require greater flexibility in the operational force, typically in the form of national caveats, in order to secure greater participation from member nations. In contrast, when national survival is at stake, like during World War II, allies are more acceptable to greater sacrifice and compromise to maintain participation lest lose an ally, namely the United States and United Kingdom's willingness to make concessions to the Soviets in exchange for their continued participation.

guidance for military forces.[5] The 1991 Strategic Concept, the first publically released, expanded the concept of security beyond just the military domain, into political, economic, social, and environmental realms.[6] Since the end of the Cold War, changes to the geostrategic landscape within which NATO was operating led to the development of another Strategic Concept 1999 (SC 99). For the first time, this concept codified the Alliance's commitment to a broader security philosophy, beyond just defense against an attack on a member nation's sovereignty. SC 99 acknowledged the requirement to be able to conduct both Collective Defense Operations (CDO) and non-Article 5 Crisis Response Operations (CRO).[7] It was, however, to be of greater importance in the conduct of the latter. This concept represents the first successful consensus to garner and maintain support for out-of-area operations.[8] Operations in Kosovo, Afghanistan and Iraq have put SC 99 to the test. Given varying national interests and threat perceptions, it has proven difficult to conduct and manage CROs. NATO is currently developing a new strategic concept, which is anticipated to be complete by the next NATO Summit in November 2010. It is expected to specifically address minimum capabilities requirements and apply an inclusive and participatory approach from the biggest to the smallest ally, reducing the friction of numerous national caveats. This concept is at the heart of the complex nature of the civil-military relations

---

[5] John R. Deni, *Alliance Management and Maintenance* (Hampshire: Ashgate Publishing Company, 2007), 32.

[6] North Atlantic Council, *Strategic Concept*, 1991, paragraph 24.

[7] Article 5 of the North Atlantic Treaty deals primarily with the defense of members of the Alliance and embodies the principle that an attack against any one of them is considered as an attack against all. Alliance activities beyond consultation, which is dealt with in Article 4 of the treaty, are referred to collectively as "Non-Article 5 Operations" SC 99 goes on to delineate them as CROs and CDOs. *The North Atlantic Treaty* (Washington D.C., April 4, 1949), http://www.nato.int/cps/en/natolive/official_texts_17120.htm (accessed July 10, 2010); North Atlantic Council, *The Alliance's Strategic Concept* (Brussels: NATO Office of Information, 24 April 1999), http://www.nato.int/cps/en/SID-CFFB8FA9-D3C6ACBF/natolive/official_texts_27433.htm (accessed July 10, 2010), paragraph 31.

[8] There are numerous examples of disputes between 1949 and 1990, where consensus was not reached or public criticism was voiced between Alliance members. For a listing, see Douglas T. Stuart, *Can NATO Transcend Its European Borders? NATO Out-of-Area Disputes* (Carlisle Barracks, PA:Strategic Studies Institute, 1991), 19-21.

within NATO and requires deliberate, transparent debate about the role of the alliance, its required capabilities and its decision-making structure.

As the International Security Assistance Force (ISAF) in Afghanistan enters its eighth year, the effectiveness of its mandate remains in question.[9] This has led to donor fatigue and a growing number of national caveats that dictate how willing participants are to prosecute campaigns. Obviously, this has large implications on the execution and potential success of these operations, and ultimately the credibility of the Alliance. Guidelines on when and where the alliance will operate outside its borders must be considered, once again bringing the debate of out-of-area operations to the foreground. Whether NATO is a global or regional alliance will depend on the political limitations that member states put on NATO's global strategic ambitions.

This monograph will examine the viability of recent NATO out-of-area operations under the current civil-military system, especially regarding strategy formulation and execution. It demonstrates that the complex decision-making bureaucracy of NATO can be a detriment to the capabilities of the organization and limits the strategic options available to the alliance. By making an investigation of these events leading up to the commitment of NATO to the ISAF and its assumption of the mission entirely, it becomes clear that these structures fail to provide a viable approach to addressing military resource commitments and the formation of a coherent strategy that meets the alliance's objectives. Through this approach, it becomes apparent that the anticipated new strategic concept must once again consider transforming its decision-making structures from a consensus model that burdens its formulation and execution of strategy, or limit

---

[9] For an few accounts of the record of the ISAF see Sean M. Maloney, *Enduring the Freedom: A Rogue Historian in Afghanistan* (Washington, DC.: Potomac Books Inc., 2005); Donald P. Wright et al., *A Different Kind of War: The United States Army in Operation ENDURING FREEDOM, October 2001 - September 2005* (Fort Leavenworth: CSI Press, 2010); Richard Rupp, *NATO after 9/11: An Alliance in Continuing Decline* (New York: Palgrave Macmillan, 2006); Vincent Morelli, "NATO in Afghanistan: A Test of the Transatlantic Alliance," Congressional Research Service, October 23, 2008; Jennifer Medcalf, *Going Global or Going Nowhere?: Nato's Role in Contemporary International Security* (New York: Peter Lang, 2008), 175-212; Sean Naylor, *Not a Good Day to Die: The Untold Story of Operation Anaconda*, 1St Edition ed. (New York: Berkley Hardcover, 2005)

its strategic ambitions in line with its regional reach, limited financial constraints and marginal political support.

This study consists of four sections. The first section describes the civil military structure of the Alliance and then expands on how these structures relate to one another in the process of strategy formulation, specifically for the Strategic Concept that NATO is currently in the process of revising. The second section examines NATO post Cold War strategy, and begins by framing it through the lens of one of the most contentious debates throughout the history of the Alliance, namely out-of-area operations. While this section summarizes this lengthy debate, it then uses operations in Kosovo to illustrate the difficulties in executing the strategy adopted by the Alliance and how it drove the first revision of NATO's Strategic Concept. It highlights limitations and restrictions of the bureaucracy and decision-making process of the Alliance. The third section moves to the ongoing and most ambitious operation of its kind for the Alliance, that of the International Security Assistance Force (ISAF) in Afghanistan. Again, demonstrating that the same struggles faced in Kosovo are only magnified by the greater distance and stresses placed on the consensus decision-making of the Alliance, this has driven the Alliance to once again revise its Strategic Concept. The final section offers some conclusions about the inefficiencies of the civil military structure of the Alliance and their inability to adopt a strategy which can then be translated into effective operations to promote its collective security. In closing, some recommendations are proposed for the development of the new Strategic Concept of the Alliance.

Structure and Strategy of the Alliance

Civil-Military Structure

In order to comprehend the process of strategy formulation for the Alliance, it is necessary to understand its civil military structures and how they relate to one another. The essential principle for alliance decision-making is consensus. Consensus is the principal characteristic and detriment of NATO's decision-making process. There is no system of voting and all decisions have to be unanimous. Extensive consultations and discussions are often required before making an important decision. Although this system is extremely slow and at times insurmountable, decreasing efficiency and timeliness, it has two major advantages in theory. First, the sovereignty and independence of each member country is respected. Second, when a decision is reached, it has the full backing of all member countries and their commitment to implement it.

NATO does not have its own independent armed forces. Most forces available to NATO remain under full national command and control until member countries assign them to carry out operations. These tasks can range from common defense to collective security, such as peacekeeping and peace-support operations like those in Kosovo or Afghanistan. The Integrated Military Structure provides the organizational framework for commanding and planning for the defense of member countries or their interests against threats to their security or stability. It consists of a network of major subordinate commands spread throughout the North Atlantic region. The role of NATO's political and military structures is to provide the political authority and joint military planning required by assigned national forces to carry out these tasks as well as the organizational arrangements needed for their joint command, control, training and exercising.[10]

---

[10] *NATO Handbook* (Brussels: NATO Office of Information Belgium, 2001), 249-251.

The basic machinery for decision-making and building consensus between the 28 nations of the alliance consists of seven fundamental elements. The most important decision-making body in NATO is the North Atlantic Council on which each member country has a permanent representative or ambassador, supported by a staff and advisers. The Council meets at ambassadorial level weekly, and there are biannual meetings of the Council at the level of Foreign Ministers, Defense Ministers and, usually at least once a year, Heads of State and Government. Appointed by the NAC for approximately four years, the Secretary General heads NATO. The Secretary General chairs meetings of the North Atlantic Council and other important NATO bodies and helps to build consensus among the member nations. In managing day-to-day activities of the Alliance, an international staff is drawn from the member countries and is tasked by the Council, Committees and Working Groups on a wide variety of pressing issues relevant to the alliance.[11]

The North Atlantic Council has established many committees and planning groups to support its work. The most essential of these are the Nuclear Planning Group, the Defense Planning Committee (DPC), and the Military Committee, meeting at different levels, either at the political headquarters of NATO in Brussels or in different member countries.[12] The Nuclear Planning Group is responsible for Alliance nuclear policy, which includes safety and security of nuclear weapons, employment planning, nuclear proliferation and nuclear arms control. Participation in this group is open to all members that are part of the integrated military structure and is not limited to those members possessing nuclear weapons. The Defense Planning Committee is the principal decision-making authority for the integrated military structure of NATO. The DPC overseas policy for all forces made available to NATO by participating member nations. Lastly, the Military Committee is the key element of NATO's military structure. It is

---

[11] *NATO Handbook*, 220-221.

[12] Ibid., 219-220.

composed of the Chiefs of Defense of NATO member countries, the International Military Staff, and the military Command Structure, which is composed of Allied Command Operations and Allied Command Transformation, headed respectively by the Supreme Allied Commander Europe (SACEUR) and the Supreme Allied Commander, Transformation (SACT).[13]

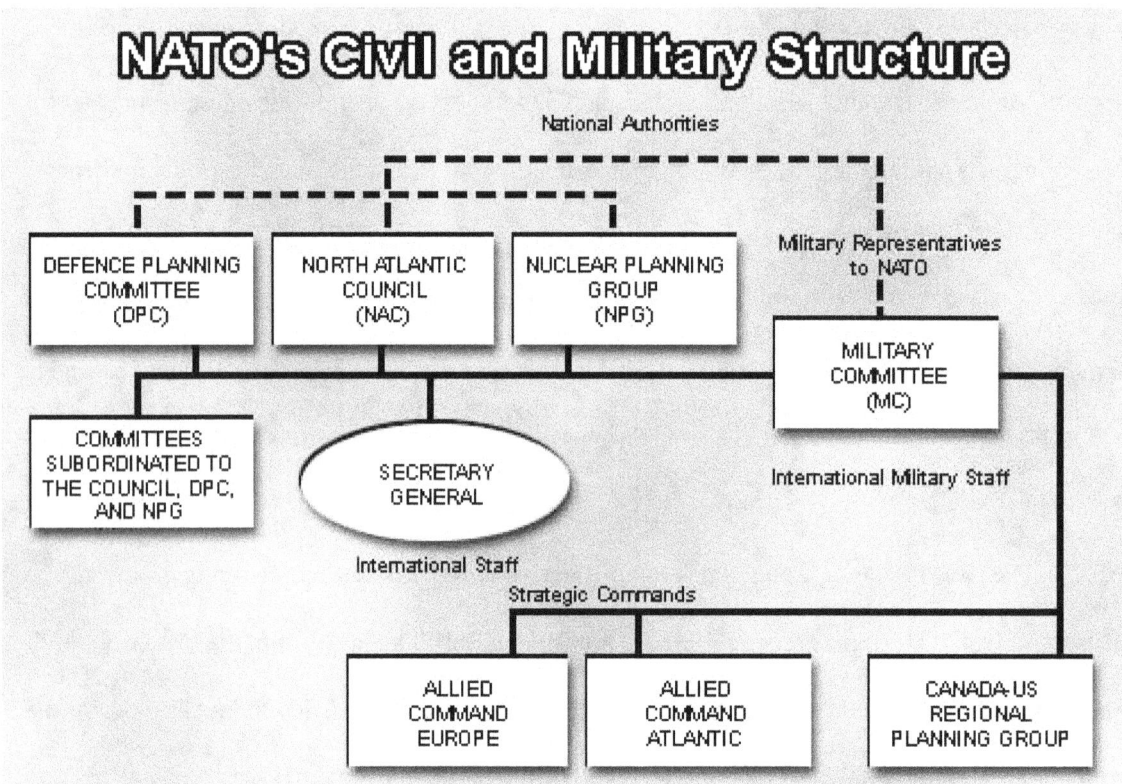

Figure 1: NATO's Civil Military Structure[14]

Forces are available for NATO operations in accordance with predetermined readiness criteria and with rules of deployment and transfer of authority to NATO command that varies from country to country, depending on national caveats. In assigning forces to NATO, member nations delegate operational command or operational control as distinct from full command over all aspects of the operations and administration of those forces. These latter aspects continue to be a national responsibility and remain under national control. In general, most NATO forces remain

---

[13] The Chairman of the Joint Chiefs of Staff (CJCS) is the representative for the United States in the Military Committee.

[14] ....

under full national command until they assigned to the Alliance for a specific operation decided upon at the political level. Additional forces may participate in operations outside of this structure, namely other coalition forces or special capabilities not specifically approved for use by the NAC.

Although the civil military structure of NATO has adapted several times throughout its history, each permutation has more often than not been to extend the political and military ties between the loose association of sovereign states in order to preserve the alliance, rather than simplify the complex decision making bureaucracy.[15] This was intentional on the part of the North Atlantic Council (NAC) in order to engage the member nations on matters outside of the realm of defense so that the alliance existence would not be dependent on the binding force of a common threat. However, over the past two decades as NATO has moved away from common defense to collective security, differing perceptions and internal interests have bogged down the organization for the very same reasons that the complex decision making processes were created in the first place. Once again, as the alliance finds its staying power in question the bureaucracy is exploring another functional and structural transformation in order to justify its existence and continue to fulfill its role to the member nations.

Civil-Military Relations and Strategy Development

How groups of leaders, civilian and military, interact and understand each other has a crucial influence on what strategy is developed and then what kind of campaign is pursued to achieve that strategy. While much has been written about civil-military relations, little of it is

---

[15] Rob De Wijk, *NATO on the Brink of the New Millennium: The Battle for Consensus*, 1st English Edition (London: Brassey's, 1997), 1-5. Stanley R. Sloan also makes a similar argument in *NATO, the European Union, and the Atlantic Community: The Transatlantic Bargain Challenged*, 2 ed. (Lanham, MD.: Rowman & Littlefield Publishers, 2005), Chapter 1.

directly relevant to alliances. [16] Stephen M. Walt has proposed a theory for justifying the existence of international alliances, and in the process explains the behavior of alliances and their member nations, but only in very general terms and predominantly in regards to their formation. [17] Once formed, how alliances operate during times of conflict requires lucid understanding of the nuances and complexities of allied relations between their institutions, always relevant to the perception of the threat. In moving from the idea of what civil-military relations should be to how civil-military relations actually work, understanding of these theorists' ideas may help explain civil-military relations in alliances, especially in developing and executing strategy in NATO.

With NATO's 60-plus year history, much is understood on its structure, decision-making process, and functionality in peacetime conditions. [18] Not surprisingly, less is understood about what happens to alliances once hostilities have begun. [19] Current literature on alliances makes two contradictory claims about burden sharing in wartime. On one hand, states will pass responsibility to their allies; while on the other hand, they will commit themselves in order to contain the threat, in doing so increase the cumulative capabilities of the alliance. [20] Varying national objectives and

---

[16] These theories include, but are not limited to, Samuel Huntington's theory on subjective versus objective civilian control, Morris Janowitz's convergence theory of a citizen soldier-based force, and Eliot Cohen's unequaled dialogue. None of the theorists speaks directly to civil military relations in alliances. However, it does not mean that their theories may not be useful in understanding alliance behavior. Eliot Cohen, *Supreme Command: Soldiers, Statesmen, and Leadership in Wartime*, First Edition ed. (New York: Free Press, 2002); Samuel P. Huntington, *The Soldier and the State: The Theory and Politics of Civil-Military Relations* (Cambridge: Belknap Press of Harvard University Press, 1981); Morris Janowitz, *The Professional Soldier: A Social and Political Portrait* (New York: Free Press, 1971).

[17] Stephen M. Walt, *The Origins of Alliances* (Ithaca: Cornell University Press, 1990), Chapter 2.

[18] David S. Yost, *NATO Transformed: The Alliances New Roles in International Security* (Washington D.C.: United States Institute of Peace, 1999), 37-72.

[19] John J. Mearsheimer, *The Tragedy of Great Power Politics* (New York: W. W. Norton & Company, 2001), 267-272; Rajan Menon, *The End of Alliances*, Reprint ed. (New York: Oxford University Press, USA, 2008), 92-95. Jeremy Pressman, *Warring Friends: Alliance Restraint in International Politics*, 2nd edition (Ithaca: Cornell University Press, 2008), 7-11; Glenn Herald Snyder, *Alliance Politics* (Ithaca: Cornell University Press, 2007), 320-28.

[20] Stephen M. Walt, *The Origins of Alliances* (Ithaca: Cornell University Press, 1990), 148-178; John J. Mearsheimer, *The Tragedy of Great Power Politics* (New York: W. W. Norton & Company, 2001), 323-329.

perception of threat between allies is one reason for this inequity in burden sharing. At the senior

levels of national leadership, the line separating military and political objectives tends to blur.

From a purely military perspective, these are distortions and distractions from the objective of

defeating the threat. However, senior military officers remain crucial participants in the process

of translating policy into strategy that their state seeks individually, and if leading the alliance

military formation, collectively.

For NATO this process of strategy formation has been convoluted and ambiguous. At its

inception and through its early years, the charter itself served as the basis for NATO policy, and

with the monolithic threat of the Soviet Union, this was initially sufficient. However, as the

security environment altered and member nations began to express divergent national interests the

charter failed to fully serve as coherent policy from which a strategy for developing alliance

capabilities and ensuring equitable burden sharing could be developed. The difficulty in forming

alliance strategy is imparting sufficient precision to be useful to the officials or forces responsible

for policy implementation, while still contributing to the deterrence of aggression and coercion

from identified threats in a predictable manner for the allies.[21]

After the end of the Cold War, there was a consensus in NATO that it was appropriate to

review Alliance strategy to match the changed international environment. Prior to 1991, the

Allies had not prepared a strategic concept since 1967, when they approved MC 14/3, generally

known as 'flexible response.' [22] In 1967, they also endorsed the Harmel Report, which set forth

the Alliance's broad political approach for relations with the Soviet Union and its Warsaw Pact

---

[21] Christopher S. Chivvis, *Recasting NATO's Strategic Concept: Possible Directions for the United States* (Santa Monica, CA.: RAND Corporation, 2010), 1-2.

[22] MC 14/3, *Overall Strategic Concept for the Defense of the North Atlantic Treaty Organization Area,* approved by the Defence Planning Committee in Ministerial Session on 12 December 1967, is available in Gregory W. Pedlow, ed., *NATO Strategy Documents 1949-1969* (Brussels: NATO Information Service, 1997), pp. 345-370.

allies.[23] The report and the ensuing strategy is credited with timely expansion of NATO's

mission, while maintaining unity and identifying common interests between the allies.[24] MC 14/3

and the Harmel Report together dealt with approximately the same areas encompassed by the

1991 Strategic Concept. The fact that the Allies did not prepare a new strategic concept from

1967 to 1991 may be attributed not only to the generality of the 1967 policy statements, but also

to the evident political difficulties involved in preparing such documents. In fact, this debate was

so drawn out and comprised such a wide-range of differing opinion, that most saw little reason to

re-open the argument over strategy development in the 1970s and 80s. Figure 2 displays the

production timeline of strategy documents for the Alliance since its founding.

Once the threat of the Soviet Union had dissolved and the alliance expanded, a strategic

concept was developed to offer latitude with regard to uncertain foreseeable security

developments, yet maintain its consensus decision-making structures. The Alliance's Strategic

Concept lies only below the North Atlantic Treaty in the hierarchy of NATO documents as an

expression of the Alliance's policy.[25] It provides a broad, open to negotiation, framework for the

range of the Alliance's pursuits and complements many other documents, including summit

statements and regular ministerial communiqués approved by the North Atlantic Council that

build upon and update each strategic concept.[26] Since its inception, the Alliance has not

---

[23] Stanley R. Sloan, *NATO, the European Union, and the Atlantic Community: The Transatlantic Bargain Challenged*, 2 ed. (Lanham, MD.: Rowman & Littlefield Publishers, 2005), 47-52. Belgian Foreign Minister Pierre Harmel was commissioned to study "The Future Tasks of the Alliance." His findings argued that NATO had not become irrelevant and reaffirmed the requirement for common defense, while at the same time encouraging greater political consultation between the member governments. This report represented the first broadening of alliance goals. Sloan draws an analogy between what the changing security environment when Harmel wrote his report and today.

[24] Ryan C. Hendrickson, *Diplomacy and War at NATO: The Secretary General and Military Action after the Cold War* (Columbia, Mo.: University of Missouri, 2006), 28.

[25] *The NATO Handbook* (Brussels: NATO Office of Information Belgium, 2001), 43.

[26] Frank R. Douglas, *The United States, NATO, and a New Multilateral Relationship (PSI Reports)* (Westport, Conn.: Praeger, 2007), 130.

developed strategic concepts regularly. They have done so only when convinced of the political and practical necessity.

Prior to 1991, the Alliance's strategic concepts were classified documents that dealt with military strategy for deterrence and corresponding force requirements for defense.[27] However, while the 1991 and 1999 Strategic Concepts were also composed with this purpose in mind, they were also intended to communicate the Alliance's strategy to their citizens and to non-allied governments in a transparent fashion. As a result, since 1991 the Alliance's strategic concepts have been unclassified statements with several purposes. Primarily, the formal concept offers a coherent framework for the Alliance's many activities, providing guidance for military policy, including operations and capabilities development, furthering public understanding of the Alliance's purpose and communicating intentions to potential adversaries, as well as current and prospective partners, across the globe. Yet, in the current era of persistent conflict, the strategic concept still fails to offer a comprehensive direction to the Alliance's purposes and plans.

Since 1991, the security environment and alliance activities have substantially changed. In the 1991 Strategic Concept the Allies acknowledged the risks of ethnic and territorial conflicts in Central and Eastern Europe. There was little expectation of performing non-Article 5 missions, such as crisis management and peacekeeping at that time. The Allies, however, have undertaken several major non-Article 5 operations, namely Operation Deliberate Force (August-September 1995), followed by NATO-led Implementation Force (IFOR) and Stabilization Force (SFOR) deployments in Bosnia, and the Operation Allied Force (March-June 1999) and the subsequent Kosovo Force (KFOR) mission.[28] The persistent out-of-area operations, though in the near abroad of the Balkans, that NATO conducted in the 1990s made the 1991 Strategic Concept seem

---

[27] Douglas, *The United States, NATO, and a New Multilateral Relationship*, 130

[28] John R. Deni, *Alliance Management and Maintenance* (Hampshire: Ashgate Publishing Company, 2007), 32.

DUE TO COPYRIGHT RESTRICTIONS
SOME OR ALL IMAGES ARE NOT INCLUDED

Figure 2: Evolution of NATO Strategy 1949-1999[29]

---

[29] Dr. Gregory Pedlow, ed., *Nato Strategy Documents 1949-1969* (Brussels, Belgium: NATO Information Service, 1997), page nr., http://www.nato.int/docu/stratdoc/eng/intro.pdf (accessed September 21, 2010).

increasingly out of step with NATO's role in the post-Cold War world. In fact, rather than anticipating the major operations of the 1990s, the 1991 Strategic Concept focused on the Alliance's Article 5 task of common defense against aggression affecting the Alliance's territory, rather than intervention beyond that territory.[30] This suggests that NATO, at least not publically, foresaw participating in any crisis management or peacekeeping operations.

---

[30] North Atlantic Council, *NATO Strategic Concept* (Brussels: 7 November 1991), paragraph 39-40.

NATO Post Cold War Strategy

Debate on Out-of-Area Operations

Alliances, if they are to be maintained involve some infringement on the autonomy of their members. Each state will try to influence the decisions of the other member states in the favor of their own national interests, while resisting those same states from meddling in their own domestic affairs and decision-making processes. Throughout NATO's history, one of the most ongoing debates between its members has been over soliciting allied support for operations beyond NATO's borders. From the challenges of European decolonization through the present, the allies have used the notion of common security interests to propose commitment of NATO forces to what today is referred to as out-of-area operations. These operations are understood to mean anywhere outside the territorial integrity of the member states.[31] Despite spurring tenacious disputes, this debate has never threatened NATO's existence and repeatedly has fostered improvement in consultation and cooperation.[32]

This ongoing debate on out-of-area operations has greater salience since the end of the Cold War. This is in part because in the 1990s, out-of-area operations, especially in NATO's near abroad, helped to justify the alliance's ongoing utility. Presently, since NATO has incorporated much of Europe, out-of-area suggests outside of the continent. Although the United Nations-sanctioned Gulf War that expelled Sadaam Hussein's forces from Kuwait was not a NATO war, the 34 countries of the coalition against Iraq included numerous NATO members and NATO bases in Germany, Italy, Portugal, Spain, and Turkey were utilized. Thus, the alliance's first major engagement outside of Europe has been their participation in the US-led invasion against

---

[31] Douglas A. Stuart, *Can NATO Transcend Its European Borders: NATO Out-of-Area Disputes* (Carlisle, PA:Strategic Studies Institue, 1991), 19-21. The appendix in this work lists all extra regional challenges to NATO solidarity from 1949 to 1990.

[32] Rebecca R. Moore, *NATO's New Mission: Projecting Stability in a Post-Cold War World* (Westport, CT.: Praeger, 2007), 33-34, 102;

Al-Qaeda and the Taliban in Afghanistan. In addition to the largest deployment of NATO in its history to serve as the International Security Assistance Force (ISAF), since 2004 the alliance has conducted counter-terrorism operations on the Eastern Mediterranean Sea, deployed 200 soldiers to Iraq to train the new Iraqi army and police, and deployed NATO warships to patrol shipping lanes off the Somali coast to counter the increasing piracy in the area in support of Operation Allied Provider.[33]

Following the September 2001 terrorist attacks on New York and Washington D.C., the Bush administration at first rejected any direct NATO involvement in the war in Afghanistan.[34] The initial combat operations to remove the Taliban from power were nearly all-American operations.[35] Nevertheless, once major hostilities had abated, international support was desired for the stabilization and reconstruction of the country. NATO was really the only viable organization that could contribute significantly to this challenge. In August 2003, after the Taliban had been toppled, NATO assumed responsibility for which included voluntary participation from fifteen non-NATO countries. The original ISAF objective was to secure Kabul and other key population centers from enemy combatants, but in October 2003 the United Nations Security Council authorized the gradual expansion of ISAF's mission throughout Afghanistan. By 2006, the entire country was a NATO operational area and the list of top ISAF

---

[33] Martin A. Smith, "Afghanistan in Context: NATO Out-of-Area Debates in the 1990s," *UNISCI Discussion Paper*, Number 22 (Madrid: University of Madrid, 2010), 17-31 at http://www.ucm.es/info/unisci.

[34] Moore, *NATO's New Mission: Projecting Stability in a Post-Cold War World*, 97-102.

[35] This monograph was largely written before its publication, but *A Different Kind of War* is the US Army's contemporary history of its campaign in Afghanistan between October 2001 and September 2005, and offers a comprehensive chronological narrative of the first four years of Operation Enduring Freedom. Donald P. Wright et al., *A Different Kind of War: The United States Army in Operation ENDURING FREEDOM, October 2001 - September 2005* (Fort Leavenworth: CSI Press, 2010)

commanders has included generals not only from the United States but also from the Canada,

France, Germany, Italy, the Netherlands, Turkey, and the United Kingdom.[36]

Winning in Afghanistan remains NATO's political and military priority.[37] Winning

means not just defeating Al-Qaeda and the Taliban insurgency, but also training and equipping an

Afghan army and police that are capable of ensuring public safety. Despite some progress,

problems linger particularly in terms of the unequal risk and burden sharing between alliance

members. The repeated statements issued from Brussels and Washington sound increasingly

hallow, and are meant only to serve the national constituencies and political interests,

inadvertently working to undermine NATO's credibility. Alliance leadership is well aware that

NATO's performance in Afghanistan is capable of jeopardizing the relevancy of the Alliance and

its ability to pursue operations outside of Europe in the future. Partially in response to this, in

early 2009 President Barack Obama ordered 17,000 fresh troops deployed in Afghanistan, adding

to the 66,000 NATO and U.S. troops already there.[38]

Operating in the harsh environment that exists in Afghanistan has been difficult. The

extreme climate, mountainous terrain and sparse, undeveloped infrastructure has challenged

NATO forces tactically. The deterioration of the security situation from an operational

perspective is related to the poorly developed strategy of the Alliance. The impediments are the

fact that member states have varying national interests at stake, are unable to decide on a clear set

---

[36] Richard Rupp, *NATO after 9/11: An Alliance in Continuing Decline* (New York: Palgrave Macmillan, 2006), 153-58.

[37] NATO, North Atlantic Council, "Bucharest Summit Declaration", Bucharest, Romania (Brussels: NATO Press Office, 2008), http://www.nato.int/cps/en/natolive/official_texts_8443.htm (accessed November 10, 2010), paragraph 6; Earlier, Jaap de Hoop Scheffer identified his priorities as Secretary General, his first being Afghanistan. Rupp, "Afghanistan Today: NATO's Last Hurrah", *NATO After 9/11: An Alliance in Decline*, 153.

[38] Military leadership had been requesting more troops in order to fight the war more effectively and to be able to consolidate gains. The 17,000 troops represent a compromise between the administration and U.S. military authorities, who would prefer a larger commitment of troops. Eric Schmitt, "Obama Issues Order for More Troops in Afghanistan," *New York Times*, November 30, 2009. http://www.nytimes.com/2009/12/01/world/asia/01orders.html (accessed October 10, 2010).

of objectives, are unwilling to compromise on threat definition and lack the will to use military force effectively. It is not likely that the alliance could have prevented the escalation in violence, but it was and remains capable of influencing their outcome. The increases in ISAF manpower is expected to yield dividends as conditions begin to improve. Some evidence suggests that one benefit of the alliance's operations in Afghanistan has been the rapidly rising effectiveness of participating NATO forces.[39] Directly contributing to NATO capabilities, several member states involved in counterinsurgency operations in some of the more challenging regions of the country have become extremely competent fighting the Taliban and securing the population.[40]

This undertaking by NATO of such a complex mission, well outside of sovereign member boundaries is testing the resolve of the alliance from both a political and military perspective. According to a recent Congressional Research Service (CRS) report for Congress, since September 11, 2001, "the allies have sought to create a "new" NATO, able to go beyond the European theater to combat new threats such as terrorism and the proliferation of weapons of mass destruction (WMD)."[41] These operations are testing the validity of SC 99 and are pushing the Alliance to its limits. Only if consensus is retained for combating security threats well beyond NATO's geographic boundaries can success be expected. The question remains how to sustain the consensus and what policy and organizational changes are required to continue these types of out of area operations well into the future, this could potentially include changes to decision-making processes and increased commitment to military capabilities. The next section will

---

[39] Vincent Morelli, "NATO in Afghanistan: A Test of the Transatlantic Alliance," Congressional Research Service, October 23, 2008, 34; Lisa Burgess, "War in Afghanistan Has Improved Nato Forces, Official Says," *Stars and Stripes*, September 15, 2006. http://www.stripes.com/news/war-in-afghanistan-has-improved-nato-forces-official-says-1.54141 (accessed November 12, 2010).

[40] Theo Farrella, "Improving in War: Military Adaptation and the British in Helmand Province, Afghanistan, 2006-2009," *Journal of Strategic Studies.* 33, no. 4 (August 2010): 567-94, http://pdfserve.informaworld.com/896024_926058792.pdf (accessed November 14, 2010).

[41] Vincent Morelli, "NATO in Afghanistan: A Test of the Transatlantic Alliance," Congressional Research Service, October 23, 2008, 2.

examine NATO's first and longest enduring out-of-area operation in order to examine difficulties in executing the strategy adopted by the Alliance and how it drove the first revision of NATO Strategic Concept.

Kosovo: Strategy Lost in Translation

During the 1990s, the disintegration of Yugoslavia led to civil wars in the Balkans. This violence cast a pallor over Europe's post-Cold War euphoria. By mid-decade, after the European Union proved ineffectual at mitigating regional hostilities, NATO became increasingly engaged in the region. In early 1998, the Federal Republic of Yugoslavia (FRY) and the Kosovo Liberation Army (KLA) entered into open armed conflict after a decade of oppressive Serb rule of ethnic Kosovar Albanians that led to violent resistance by the KLA.[42] In response to KLA successes throughout much of the province, the Yugoslav government launched a major counteroffensive, which continued through the summer. The war displaced over a quarter of a million people, destroyed thousands of homes, and confronted the international community with a humanitarian disaster.[43] Diplomatic negotiations continued through the spring of 1999, but neither the Holbrooke Agreement nor Rambouillet Strategy succeeded in producing a long lasting cessation of hostilities and fighting on the ground in Kosovo escalated by March 1999.[44]

A unilateral approach to the crisis would have proved far costlier than any single country was willing to bear. Despite widespread public feeling in Europe that the FRY should not be allowed to conduct an ethnic cleansing campaign against the Kosovars, no states in Europe had sufficient capabilities to intervene unilaterally. Attributed to decades of low defense budgets and limited capacity, the European member states were unable to take action without the strategic

---

[42] In 2003, it was reconstituted as a political union called the State Union of Serbia and Montenegro. Ivo H. Daalder and Michael E. O'Hanlon, *Winning Ugly: Nato's War to Save Kosovo* (Washington, D.C.: Brookings Institution Press, 2001), 22-23.

[43] Ibid., 40-42.

[44] Ibid., 45-89.

assets of the United States. Because of reluctance on the part of the countries to act alone, acting

via NATO was the only viable and least costly option. The NATO member states ultimately

agreed that ending the brutality in Kosovo was obligatory, but even coming to that agreement was

difficult. By January 1999, the member states of NATO had finally agreed to use air strikes to

compel the FRY into capitulation. After lengthy planning, the air campaign, Operation Allied

Force, began 23 March 1999 and lasted until 10 June. This campaign brought an end to the FRY

military operations, though it took much longer than expected.[45] NATO troops have remained in

Kosovo following the 1999 air campaign and even after the declaration of the province's

independence in February 2008.

The Kosovo campaign was the first time NATO's military command and decision-

making bureaucracy conducted an actual war. Despite the long history of alliance cooperation,

prosecuting the war in Kosovo proved very challenging for NATO.[46] NATO's concern of further

violence in the Balkans and the effects it would have in regional stability was at odds, while a

commitment to NATO and keeping the alliance active were important considerations as well.[47]

The uncertainty in the alliance resulted from divergent perspectives, with many member states

having different perspectives on the threat posed by the conflict and what action should be taken.

The alliance struggled to agree on exactly how to stop FRY aggression. These varying

perspectives were for a variety of reasons, shared cultural background with the Kosovar

Albanians, historic ties to ';the FRY, internal government conflicts, varied national interests and

potential for Yugoslavian retaliation.[48]

---

[45] Benjamin S. Lambeth, *NATO's Air War for Kosovo: A Strategic and Operational Assessment* (Washington: RAND, 2001), 8-10.

[46] Wesley Clark, *Waging Modern War: Bosnia, Kosovo, and the Future of Combat* (New York: Public Affairs, 2002), 168-69.

[47] Eliot A. Cohen, "Kosovo and the New American Way of War," *War Over Kosovo*, ed. Andrew J. Bacevich and Eliot A. Cohen (New York: Columbia University Press, 2002), 46.

[48] Clark, *Waging Modern War: Bosnia, Kosovo, and the Future of Combat*, 170.

Waging coalition warfare is extremely difficult. Even Clausewitz understood this when he posed the question of whether states are pursuing their own interests with their own means or whether their interests and forces are combined under some degree of political unity.[49] While alliance partners agreed on general goals, it was difficult to agree on a strategy toward attaining those goals. In fact, the absence of clear military objectives was one of the principal departures from military doctrine in Operation Allied Force.[50] With the crises escalating, the Alliance moved quickly to build the necessary consensus, leading to vague, unclear objectives that required further detailed planning from military leadership, which was again subject to civilian approval. The contrast between Secretary General Solana's statement that the purpose of the operation is to prevent continued repression and violence against the Kosovar population and that of President Clinton is evidence of the difficulty in forming allied objectives. President Clinton stated:

> Our strikes have three objectives: First, to demonstrate the seriousness of NATO's opposition to aggression and its support for peace. Second, to deter President Milosevic from continuing and escalating his attacks on helpless civilians by imposing a price for those attacks. And, third, if necessary, to damage Serbia's capacity to wage war against Kosovo in the future by seriously diminishing its military capabilities.[51]

NATO was clearly the most logical choice to carry out operations, but their execution was constrained and inefficient due to unsound strategy that required nearly daily approval from collective civilian leadership whose decisions had to be made by consensus.[52] This was further complicated by the parallel command structure that was employed, due primarily to resistance from the United States to place its forces under the command of another member nation. The

---

[49] Carl von Clausewitz, *On War*, ed. Michael Howard and Peter Paret (Princeton: Princeton University Press, 1989), 596.

[50] This report identifies seven departures from military doctrine to include: lacking clear military objective, restrained strategic attack, inability to plan effects due to limited guidance, inability to mass through simultaneity, unsupported air interdiction, limited military flexibility, and poorly trained joint staff. GAO, "Kosovo Air Operations: Need to Maintain Alliance Cohesion Resulted in Doctrinal Departures," GAO-01-784 (Washington: GAO, 2001), 6.

[51] Cohen, "Kosovo and the New American Way of War," *War Over Kosovo*, 51.

[52] Lambeth, *NATO's Air War for Kosovo*, 185, 207.

chain of command was confusing, with unsuitable organizational structures and insufficient staff integration. According to Supreme Allied Commander Europe (SACEUR) GEN Wesley Clark, who led NATO's campaign, the operation was plagued from the start by a restrictive targeting process, operational security leaks and flawed unity of command.[53] (Figure 3)

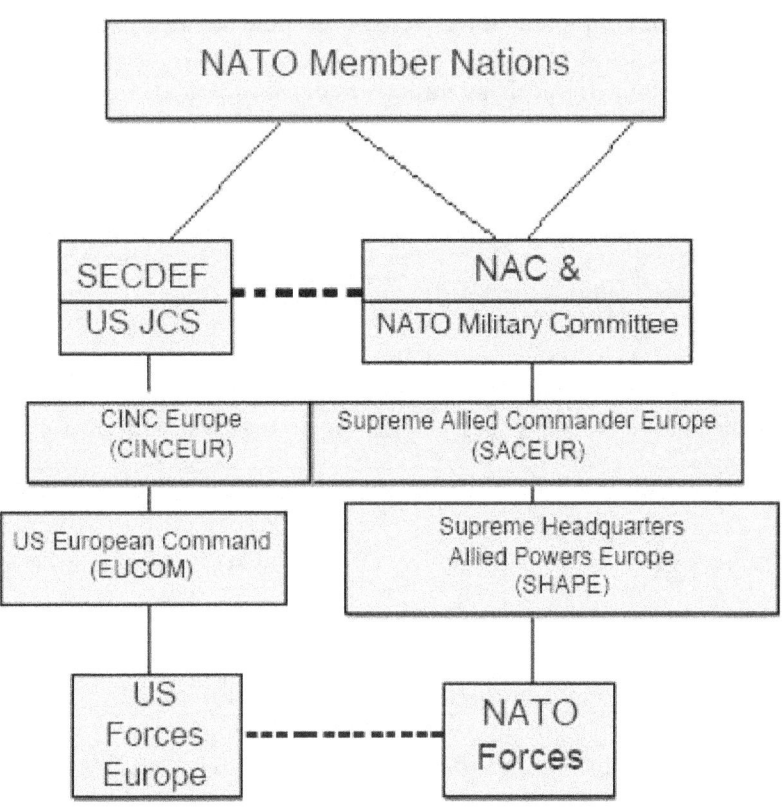

Figure 3: Command in NATO[54]

General Clark was at the nexus of decision-making during the Kosovo conflict. Serving as the focal point for strategic decision-making, he tried to use his position to influence member

---

[53] Clark, *Waging Modern War: Bosnia, Kosovo, and the Future of Combat*, 163-164, 175-176, 442, 449-450.

[54] Ian Hope, "Unity of Command in Afghanistan: A Foresaken Principle of War," *Strategic Studies Institute* (November 2008): 7, http://www.StrategicStudiesInstitute.army.mil/ (accessed August 20, 2010).

nations' civilian leadership, despite the structures of the Alliance limiting his autonomy. Clark carried much of the burden of negotiating with the multiple governments that contributed forces to the coalition battle, some of his most fierce being with his own US government. The President and the Secretary of Defense seemed remarkably detached from the conduct of operations. Contributing to the confusion, the U.S. Joint Chiefs of Staff only constrained Clark and his staff as they tried to interpret the conflicting objectives between the member nations. The shaping of alliance strategy and action by political and military authorities was a process of constant negotiation, rather than from an authoritative or advisory role. In defense of NATO member states, when conflict is more political than existential, as was the case in Kosovo, they naturally want as much time to weigh options and reflect on implications, despite the urging of military authorities to choose a course of action and act upon it.

The consequences of NATO's decision-making process was particularly apparent in the targeting process, which required all proposed targets to be reviewed, vetted and approved by NATO. Each member nation was able to veto any target. This was a lengthy process as nations evaluated each proposal for compliance with international law and the potential for collateral damage. [55] In addition to being unwieldy and slow, the alliance suffered from leaks from member governments and from within the Headquarters itself. [56] These complications revealed the difficulties among the allies in agreeing on objectives and a strategy to attain them. They also illustrated the problems associated with multinational command structure, even in long-standing, highly institutionalized alliance such as NATO. In sum, the alliance never achieved consensus on objectives or how to prosecute the war. Cohesion was so difficult to maintain that it resulted in

---

[55] Lambeth, *NATO's Air War for Kosovo*, 207.

[56] Clark, *Waging Modern War: Bosnia, Kosovo, and the Future of Combat*, 175–76.

profound departures from military doctrine, further complicating the campaign.[57] This represents one of the many inherent challenges to alliance war fighting. Despite the fact that NATO was a long-standing alliance, determining an effective strategy in wartime remained difficult.

Clark, a brilliant, politically sophisticated, and assertive soldier, exercised perhaps disproportionate or at least unusual influence over a foreign policy establishment at home that had reluctantly sent American forces off to prosecute limited engagements.[58] What seems, in all events, to have dropped out of the civilian-military dialogue was a presentation of different options and a debate among military authorities about the best course of action, conducted in the presence and for the ultimate benefit of the Alliance's civilian leadership. Clark was restrained in both formulation and execution by the vague objectives identified by the Alliance. Clark's struggle in pursuing operations against the FRY foreshadowed NATO's current conflict in Afghanistan in terms of similar inefficiencies and problematic restraint of Alliance forces.

Strategic Concept 1999

In May of 1997, as part of the Founding Act on Mutual Relations, Cooperation and Security between NATO and the Russian Federation, the Alliance announced that it would review its Strategic Concept in order to ensure that it was consistent with the challenges of the contemporary security environment.[59] This review was justified by the many new policies NATO had adopted since 1991, international circumstances, and ongoing NATO operations in the

---

[57] GAO, "Kosovo Air Operations: Need to Maintain Alliance Cohesion Resulted in Doctrinal Departures," GAO-01-784 (Washington: GAO, 2001), 3; Jan Hoekema, NATO Parliamentary Assembly, "NATO Policy and NATO Strategy in Light of the Kosovo Conflict" (Brussels: NATO Press Office, October 6, 1999), http://www.nato-pa.int/archivedpub/comrep/1999/as252dsc-e.asp (accessed November 4, 2010), paragraphs 19-26.

[58] Secretary of State, Madaline Albright was less reluctant to commit ground forces than much of the Clinton administration, the Secretary of Defense and many NATO member states. *Waging Modern War: Bosnia, Kosovo, and the Future of Combat*, 170-71, 253, 386-387.

[59] NATO, Founding Act on Mutual Relations, Cooperation and Security between NATO and the Russian Federation signed in Paris, France, May 27, 1997, http://www.nato.int/cps/en/natolive/official_texts_25468.htm (accessed November 14, 2010), paragraph 4.

Balkans.[60] Redefinition of the Alliance's fundamental security tasks was the most significant feature of the 1999 Strategic Concept. Three missions remained essentially unchanged from the 1991 to the 1999 Strategic Concepts: serve as a forum for consultation, provide for common defense, and guarantee a stable Euro-Atlantic security environment. To address the Alliance's principal new activities, the 1999 Strategic Concept listed two additional fundamental security tasks: crisis management, including conflict prevention and crisis response operations, and partnership, including dialogue and cooperation, with other states in the Euro-Atlantic region. The former marked the clearest commitment of the Alliance for an out-of-area role.

The Allies avoided resolving the issue of legitimacy in using force for non-Article 5 operations without an explicit mandate from the UN Security Council when they composed the 1999 Strategic Concept. Yet, to support its two newly outlined tasks, NATO reiterated its offer to support peacekeeping and other operations on a case-by-case basis through making available Alliance resources and expertise under the authority of the UN Security Council or the Organization for Security and Co-operation in Europe (OSCE).[61] While the Allies sanctioned out-of-area operations authorized by the UN, they also affirmed their use of force in the Kosovo and in the Balkans. This left open the possibility to conduct military operations justified on grounds of humanitarian necessity or other special interests when consensus was attained.[62] Despite the language of SC 99, some allies stated that the conflict in Kosovo did not establish any precedent,

---

[60] David S. Yost, *NATO Transformed: The Alliances New Roles in International Security* (Washington D.C.: United States Institute of Peace, 1999), 284-285.

[61] North Atlantic Council, "The Alliance's Strategic Concept," 24 April 1999, http://www.nato.int/cps/en/SID-CFFB8FA9-D3C6ACBF/natolive/official_texts_27433.htm (accessed July 10, 2010), paragraph 31.

[62] Ibid., paragraphs 3, 12 and 31.

and asserted that each ally was responsible for justifying their own participation on humanitarian grounds or UN Security Council resolutions.[63]

The last third of the 1999 Strategic Concept identified missions for NATO forces, described the characteristics of both conventional and nuclear forces, and established guidelines for their posture and readiness. It called for NATO forces to be identified and prepared to operate beyond NATO's borders. Specifically, capabilities for dealing with risks had to remain flexible, mobile, rapidly deployable and sustainable. In being prepared for both non-Article 5 operations and supporting common defense they would contribute to regional stability, promote common security interests of Alliance members and to the maintenance of peace in the Euro-Atlantic area.[64] In addition, the strategic concept emphasizes the indispensable part that Alliance forces play in addressing the danger associated with the proliferation of nuclear, biological and chemical weapons and their means of delivery. Although the concept endorses a role for nuclear forces in deterring WMD proliferation, it clearly states NATO's nuclear forces will no longer target any specific country.[65]

The 1999 Strategic Concept represented an evolutionary modification that captured the ongoing policies already adopted by the Alliance, conveyed the need for NATO to operate beyond its territorial boundaries, and proposed transformational structural changes needed to enhance force readiness. Although still relatively broad in its language, it was more detailed than the previous concept and officially expanded Alliance activities into crisis management and building partnerships. Most importantly, the 1999 Strategic Concept validated the concept of

---

[63] David S. Yost, "NATO's 1999 Strategic Concept" in *Security Strategies: NATO, the United States and the European Union* (Rome, IT: NATO Defense College, 2005), p. 24-26.

[64] North Atlantic Council, *The Alliance's Strategic Concept*, 24 April 1999, http://www.nato.int/cps/en/SID-CFFB8FA9-D3C6ACBF/natolive/official_texts_27433.htm (accessed July 10, 2010), paragraphs 47-61.

[65] Ibid., paragraph 64.

being able to project military power beyond Europe.[66] Although Kosovo revealed some of the challenges related to projecting power, it also proved the Alliance could operate beyond its original purpose of common defense.

---

[66] Frank R. Douglas, *The United States, NATO, and a New Multilateral Relationship* (Westport, Conn.: Praeger, 2007), 131-132.

Alliance Strategy for the Global War on Terror

The Evolution of ISAF

Afghanistan, which was considered the staging area for the terrorists that struck the United States on September 11, 2001, became the primary target of subsequent American military operations. NATO allies invoked Article 5 to help the US defeat the Taliban and Al Qaeda in Afghanistan as a demonstration of solidarity within the Alliance.[67] Nevertheless, the US chose to utilize the indigenous opposition forces and American air supremacy to quickly dismantle the regime without involving its allies. The US-led effort, known as Operation Enduring Freedom (OEF), had unparalleled international support because of the direct link that was drawn between Afghanistan as a safe haven for terrorist networks and the Al Qaeda attacks on the United States. Thus, while toppling the Taliban regime in Afghanistan afforded an opportunity for solidarity between NATO allies, the US's refusal to fully engage the Alliance from the beginning quickly squandered this temporary common cause to rally around.[68]

At its commencement, OEF command fell upon Commander of U.S. Central Command (CENTCOM). In the absence of a strategic forum like NATO, CENTCOM also assumed lead role in coalition management, similar to the first Persian Gulf War. This 'Coalition of the Willing' initially aroused little political opposition to a CENTCOM lead because unity garnered from the events of September 11th and from the assumption that operations in Afghanistan would be short and decisive. By mid-November 2001, after the initial military operations had led to the

---

[67] North Atlantic Council, Press Statement, 11 September 2001, available online at: http://www.nato.int/cps/en/natolive/official_texts_18863.htm; this statement was reaffirmed on 2 October 2001, after the results of investigations into the 11 September terrorist attacks against the United States clearly determined that Al-Qaida carried out the attacks, North Atlantic Council, Press Statement, 2 October 2001, available online at: http://www.nato.int/docu/update/2001/1001/e1002a.htm.

[68] Rupp, "Afghanistan Today: NATO's Last Hurrah," *NATO After 9/11: An Alliance in Decline*, 162.

collapse of the Taliban government, a UN resolution for international stability operations and rebuilding efforts was secured.

In December 2001, the Bonn Conference authorized the International Security Assistance Force (ISAF) to maintain security in Kabul to permit the transitional government to operate in relative safety.[69] This originally became an independent British-led mission to secure the post-conflict transition of Kabul only. ISAF had no command relationship with the U.S. led Combined Forces Command-Afghanistan.[70] In August 2003, after nearly two years of no formal association and months of negotiations involving the ISAF, NATO member states, and the United Nations, NATO agreed to take command and responsibility for the ISAF.[71] In October 2003, the UN Security Council expanded the ISAF mandate to the entire country of Afghanistan, with the Secretary General supporting the expansion of NATO's mission there.[72] In December 2003, the North Atlantic Council authorized the Supreme Allied Commander, General James Jones, to initiate the expansion of ISAF. Beginning in 2004, NATO assumed responsibility for the northern part of the country, then the western part of Afghanistan in 2005, and all territory in Afghanistan by late 2006.[73]

---

[69] The Bonn Conference was a meeting between anti-Taliban allies and regional leaders, to begin the process of reconstructing the country and establishing an Afghan Transitional Authority. Stanley Sloan, "NATO in Afghanistan" *UNISCI Discussion Paper*, Number 22 (Madrid: University of Madrid, 2010), http://www.ucm.es/info/unisci (accessed August 30, 2010), 35-44.

[70] David W. Barno, "Fighting 'the Other War': Counterinsurgency Strategy in Afghanistan, 2003-2005," *Military Review*, September/October 2007, p 34.

[71] Rupp, "Afghanistan Today: NATO's Last Hurrah," *NATO After 9/11: An Alliance in Decline*, 155-158.

[72] United Nations Security Council, "Resolution 1510 (2003)" 13 October 2003, http://www.nato.int/isaf/topics/mandate/unscr/resolution_1510.pdf (Accessed November 14, 2010)

[73] NATO Headquarters, "Nato's Role in Afghanistan," North Atlantic Treaty Organization, http://www.nato.int/cps/en/natolive/topics_8189.htm (accessed September 10, 2010).

Initially the relationship between the ISAF and OEF missions was not clarified. From a strategic perspective, no one was in charge of the overall Afghanistan mission.[74] This was further complicated with NATO's assumption of ISAF. The command and control of ISAF moved to NATO Joint Forces Command (JFC) Brunssum and then to Supreme Headquarters Allied Powers Europe (SHAPE), both located in Europe.[75] As in Kosovo, unity of command and political oversight of multinational forces immediately surfaced as issues with the expansion of ISAF. In order to foster greater participation from NATO member states, ISAF command rotated between different countries every six months as a designated NATO corps headquarters assumed the mission. This meant there was no continuity in command and little progress in establishing a standing relationship with the independent, ongoing US operations. Although NATO assumed operational responsibility for ISAF, SACEUR was still not the combatant commander that the United States held accountable, nor was his regional command the supporting headquarters for Afghanistan. Each of the supporting component commands remained under the control of CENTCOM. (Figure 4)

Despite many member states' hesitation to increase troop commitments and fear of increased casualties, NATO assumed the lead in Afghanistan. This decision was regarded as a positive development by the time of NATO's annual meeting in Riga in November 2006. By taking command and control of troops already deployed in the country, NATO attempted to effectively combine the US and ISAF missions which had been essentially operating in parallel since 2001. NATO's dominant role in Afghanistan was deemed as another shift in the Alliance's

---

[74] Hope, Ian. "Of Command in Afghanistan: A Foresaken Principle of War," U.S. Army War College, 2008. In Strategic Studies Institute, http://www.strategicstudiesinstitute.army.mil/pdffiles/pub889.pdf (accessed August 22, 2010). 10.

[75] Ibid., 10

aspiration to face the challenges that lie beyond Europe's borders and support it with military

force.[76]

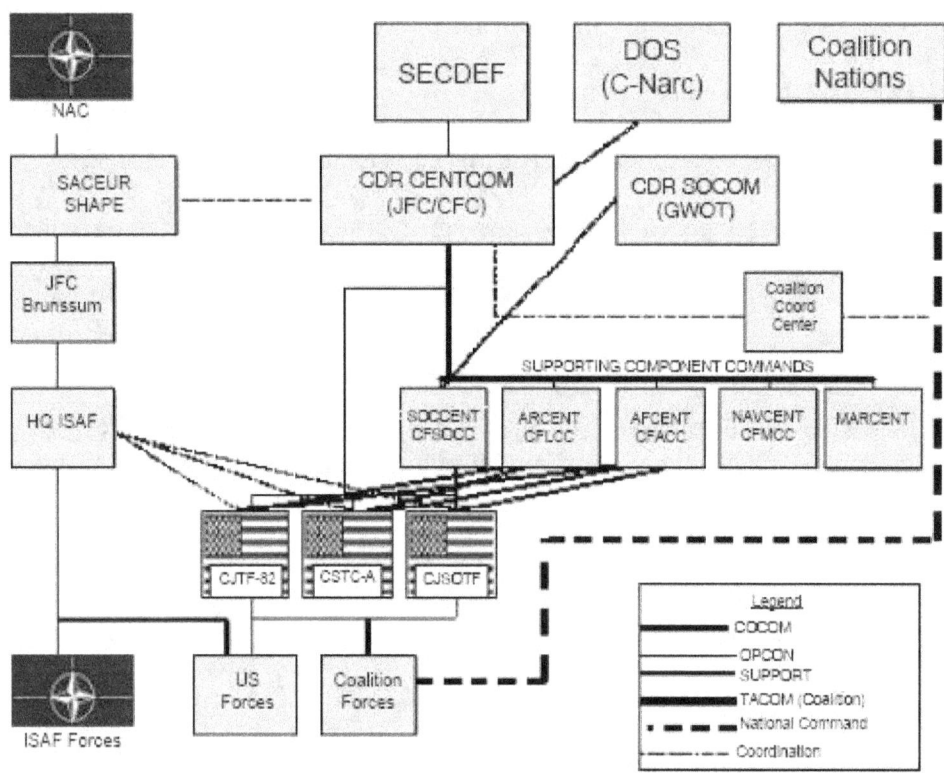

Figure 4: Command in Afghanistan[77]

NATO Strategic and Operational Challenges

While Operation Enduring Freedom was considered militarily successful, the security

situation in Afghanistan remained volatile and deteriorated significantly over time. The intent was

---

[76] NATO, North Atlantic Council, "Riga Summit Declaration," Riga, Latvia (Brussels: NATO Press Office, 2006), http://www.nato.int/cps/en/SID-63D387E5-29A1F29D/natolive/official_texts_37920.htm (accessed November 14, 2010)

[77] Hope, Ian. "Of Command in Afghanistan: A Foresaken Principle of War," U.S. Army War College, 2008. In Strategic Studies Institute, http://www.strategicstudiesinstitute.army.mil/pdffiles/pub889.pdf (accessed August 22, 2010). 11.

for NATO to shift responsibility for overall security in Afghanistan from the United States to Alliance control. The lengthy transition between U.S. and NATO responsibility permitted a reconstituted and restructured Taliban regime to gain at least coercive influence over many of the provinces of the country from their bases on the along the Afghanistan border with the northwestern provinces of Pakistan. As NATO took over in Afghanistan, it had a force of over 21,000 men from 36 different nations. As highlighted by US General James Jones, then SACEUR commander, this represents NATO's most ambitious operation, if only for the strategic distance that it spans.[78] NATO placed its reputation on the line in Afghanistan. In these circumstances, ongoing U.S. operations in Iraq, always a matter of friction between the U.S. and some of its NATO allies, exacerbated difficulties within NATO about how to proceed in Afghanistan. Any distraction from this operation was seen as a further threat to unity of the allies and the viability of the Alliance.[79]

Once NATO had responsibility for all of Afghanistan, the growing insurgency, previously ignored as an American problem, became an ISAF predicament. This was especially true as the number of Alliance casualties began to grow. At the 2004 Istanbul Summit the heads of state expanded NATO's mission in Afghanistan, but little progress has been made since that time.[80] Establishing security remained a precondition and the key to successful reconstruction in Afghanistan. After the signing of the Dayton Peace Accords in 1995, NATO deployed a force of about 60,000 troops to Bosnia to maintain peace and provide security. Afghanistan, a country nearly thirteen times the size, with a population of more than six times the size of Bosnia, initially

---

[78] NATO Press Conference August 11, 2003.

[79] Rupp, "Afghanistan Today: NATO's Last Hurrah", *NATO After 9/11: An Alliance in Decline*, Chapter 5.

[80] NATO, North Atlantic Council, "The Istanbul Declaration - Our security in a new era," Istanbul, Turkey (Brussels: NATO Press Office, 28 June 2004), http://www.nato.int/cps/en/natolive/news_52837.htm (accessed November 4, 2010)

received under half that number of troops. There has been a disconnect between the realities on the ground in Afghanistan and NATO's deployment. [81]

Rather than rushing out of Afghanistan and viewing the NATO decision as cover for an exit strategy, the US considered it an unique and historic opportunity for America and Europe to prioritize and guarantee the future security and reconstruction of Afghanistan under the control of the Alliance, thus ensuring NATO's future relevance. The US remained NATO's most important member and leader, yet in recent years in Afghanistan the US has begun to view NATO as somehow detached from itself and its own forces. In other words, the operational requirements of the security environment in Afghanistan do not match the strategic limitations placed on many NATO forces due to national caveats and casualty aversion. [82]

NATO remains unwilling to pressure member states to ease restraints, despite appeals from Alliance military leadership in order to gain greater operational flexibility. In order to compensate for this, the Obama administration decided to execute a surge of forces to meet the increasing security needs in order to buy time to build Afghan security capabilities. Despite the troop increase recently ordered by the Obama administration, there remains a troop deficit, especially in light of scheduled withdrawals of some NATO allied forces. [83] NATO cannot replace the U.S., rather it should seek to compliment and combine U.S. and European interests in Afghanistan. With continued efforts by the Obama administration, there appears to be a new

---

[81] Initially in Afghanistan there was an argument for a small footprint, lest a Mujahedeen-style resistance emerge. David Rohde and David E. Sanger, "How a 'Good War' in Afghanistan Went Bad," *New York Times*, August 12, 2007. http://www.nytimes.com/2007/08/12/world/asia/12afghan.html?pagewanted=all (accessed November 18, 2010).

[82] Michael Ruehle, "Changing Policy or Staying the Course," *World Security Network*, June 11, 2007, http://www.worldsecuritynetwork.com/showArticle3.cfm?article_id=14497 (accessed October 10, 2010)

[83] President Barack Obama, "The Way Forward in Afghanistan and Pakistan," Remarks by the President in Address to the Nation, West Point, NY, December 1, 2009. http://www.whitehouse.gov/the-press-office/remarks-president-address-nation-way-forward-afghanistan-and-pakistan (accessed November 20, 2010).

willingness to work through transatlantic issues. This may be attributed to a variety of reasons, but NATO appears to be out of its defense only mindset, realizing that facing challenges outside its immediate geography is pertinent to ensuring security within. With around 20,000 peacekeepers in the Balkans and its largest presence in Afghanistan, NATO finds itself historically forward deployed at unprecedented levels.

Yet there is considerable risk in assuming that the training of the Afghan army will produce a military force able to defend itself singlehandedly against a resurgent Taliban and conglomerate of jihadist terrorists, particularly when these forces have sanctuary in Pakistan. Given Pakistan's historic sympathy for the Taliban it is difficult to imagine Pakistan expelling these forces unless pressured to do so by the US and Europe. And even then, given the geostrategic importance of keeping Afghanistan sovereign and defeating the insurgency elements throughout the country, it is politically impossible to imagine an Afghan force ever entering Pakistan in pursuit of insurgents, whereas the US has been actively utilizing various pursuit agreements in the mountainous border region of Afghanistan and Pakistan. The US has taken an active role both in NATO and on the ground in Afghanistan to ensure the success of NATO's self declared mission, or risk driving NATO right back to isolation in Europe.

Despite these hurdles and setbacks, NATO has contributed to progress in Afghanistan.[84] To date, however, NATO's pronouncements have not matched the organization's actual accomplishments. NATO continues to paint an overly optimistic picture, in what many consider a deteriorating security environment. Some of the difficulty can certainly be attributed to a resurgent Taliban and other insurgent forces. In any case, this does not bode well for NATO's future in Afghanistan, or other out-of-area operations. Contrary to the Alliance's many public statements focusing on the importance of Afghanistan, Alliance members have not prioritized the

---

[84] Frank Cook, NATO Parliamentary Assembly, "Afghanistan: Assessing Progress and Key Challenges for the Alliance" (Brussels: NATO Press Office, 28 June 2007), http://www.nato-pa.int/default.Asp?SHORTCUT=1166 (accessed October 10, 2010)

mission and have been slow to deploy forces and tackle the readily identifiable issues that will determine NATO's success or failure in the country.[85] Despite official European communications to the contrary, it is interesting to note that most European governments still do not portray Afghanistan as a matter of national interest while in America, Afghanistan was largely overshadowed by the situation in Iraq, and only recently became the priority for the new administration. There appears to be varying positions on Afghanistan, one for domestic and one for international consumption. Amid such concerns and doubts, the expansion of ISAF not only tests European military effectiveness but also the political will in its capitals to sustain the first major NATO mission launched outside its traditional Euro-Atlantic borders.

Thus as a historic first for NATO, the Allies have more at stake in Afghanistan than their own national interests. Securing Afghanistan's future could determine the future relevance of the Alliance. A success reaffirms NATO's role as the primary military framework in which Europe and America can actively pursue their common security interests. While a failure in Afghanistan will tarnish NATO's role as a provider of peacekeeping forces and security missions throughout the globe, and seriously diminish the importance of NATO beyond its traditional Article 5 mission. Success in Afghanistan clearly requires a revised strategy and the sufficient resources to implement it, both in the US and NATO, collectively.

Strategic Concept 2010

In the context of the ongoing NATO efforts in Afghanistan, the Alliance has undertaken its third major review of its strategic concept since the end of the Cold War.[86] A sound transatlantic consensus on NATO's roles and missions and on its strategy to deal with

---

[85] Rupp, "Afghanistan Today: NATO's Last Hurrah", *NATO After 9/11: An Alliance in Decline*, 179.

[86] This monograph was completed prior to the Lisbon Summit and the release of the 2010 Strategic Concept for the Alliance.

contemporary and future security challenges is essential if NATO is to function optimally and remain viable. The Strategic Concept is a core NATO document that ideally establishes and reflects this transatlantic consensus. As the security environment that NATO has to deal with changes, so the Alliance's strategic concept has to be periodically updated. The current concept dates from 1999, a time when NATO had 19 members compared to the 28 it has today and when NATO's focus was very much on challenges within Europe or on Europe's immediate periphery.

The new Strategic Concept, which must be approved by all 28 current allies, has to take account of the way in which security challenges have evolved. These challenges include proliferation, failed states, piracy, energy supplies, terrorism, and climate change. The concept should take into account how NATO has adapted and transformed in the last decade to be able to better tackle these challenges. It will also need to give specific guidance, typically in supporting classified documents, to NATO governments on how they need to further transform their own national defense structures and capabilities to be successful in meeting NATO's core tasks in the 21st century. Finally, the Strategic Concept should give public opinion in the Alliance countries a clear sense of why NATO still matters and how it makes them more secure.

At the NATO Summit in Strasbourg in April 2009, NATO's Heads of State and Government tasked the Secretary General to develop a new NATO Strategic Concept to be completed for the next Summit, scheduled for the end of 2010.[87] The Secretary General was instructed to convene a broad based group of qualified experts to examine the current Strategic Concept and make recommendations for updating it to fit the contemporary security environment. Under the active supervision of the NAC, the development of the new Strategic Concept is to include all Allies and was also expected to engage the Euro-Atlantic Partnership Council, the Mediterranean Dialogue and the Istanbul Cooperation Initiative, as well as other global partners

---

[87] NATO, North Atlantic Council, "Strasbourg / Kehl Summit Declaration," Strasbourg, France (Brussels: NATO Press Office, 2009), http://www.nato.int/cps/en/natolive/news_52837.htm (accessed November 4, 2010)

around the globe, like Australia and Israel. Lastly, they were directed to include other key international actors such as the EU, the UN and other NGOs in the strategic community who can contribute expertise to the process in order to increase transparency.

The Group of Experts, chaired by former U.S. Secretary of State Madeleine K. Albright, was formed in early September 2009.[88] The group divided its task into two phases. The first phase, known as the reflection phase, ran from September 2009 to mid-February 2010. It was devoted to engaging the broader strategic community and policy makers in a dialogue on the challenges facing the Alliance. The second phase, the consultation phase, involved the Group of Experts travelling to each NATO capital to present the results of the Group's internal deliberations and preliminary conclusions directly to NATO governments, receiving their initial comments and feedback. The group met periodically with the Secretary General, who had overall authority over the Group's work, and with the North Atlantic Council and other stakeholders at NATO Headquarters.

Having completed their task, the Group of Experts submitted to the NAC their analysis and recommendations. They reinforced the need for NATO to develop a new strategy due to the changed global security environment since its last strategic concept, highlighting the need for timely intelligence sharing, out-of-area forces deployment, and continued planning for defense. Additionally, they identified several other areas that require comprehensive, collective strategy in order decrease risk and lessen their impact on member nation's perceptions and commitments.[89] Moreover, as the Alliance has expanded to twenty-eight nations, considerations must be taken with regard to NATO's capabilities, both present and future, and its commitments.

---

[88] NATO Headquarters, "A Roadmap for the New Strategic Concept," NATO's New Strategic Concept, http://www.nato.int/strategic-concept/roadmap-strategic-concept.html#guiding (accessed July 10, 2010).

[89] These areas include global nuclear non-proliferation regime, instability near Europe's periphery, cyber defense, piracy, energy supply, concerns about the environment and the ongoing worldwide economic crisis.

The Group of Experts also pointed out the importance of communicating the purpose of this new strategy to three main groups. First, the member nation populations must remain informed about the alliance and its relevance to their individual security in order to retain their support and ultimately their financial backing. Since the value of the Alliance may not be as obvious when the threat is not seen as existential and efforts must be made to highlight its many contributions to international stability and peace. Secondly, the process of writing a new Strategic Concept must engage member nation governments to secure the political will to support the Alliance through proportionate contributions, both monetary and capabilities. Competing national interests threaten the cohesion of the Alliance, with this in mind, they are clear to state, "the new Strategic Concept must clarify both what NATO should be doing for each Ally and what each Ally should be doing for NATO."[90] Lastly, the new concept must convey to the international community the resolve and unity of the Alliance. The purpose of this message is to deter existing threats that any challenge will be confronted and that the Alliance understands its role to ensure security as part of a global community. This is not to say that they will take on any global issue, but only that it understands its position as the most capable security organization.

The report from the Group of Experts details the current security environment, both globally and regionally. The report points out that conventional threats are unlikely, instead focusing attention on unconventional threats, namely ballistic missiles, terrorism and cyber attacks.[91] In order to combat these threats and ensure security, the Group identifies four core tasks and the capabilities to fulfill them: maintain the ability to deter and defend member states, contribute to the security of the region, act as a forum for consultation and crisis management, and foster partnerships. Expanding on this fourth core task, they stress the importance of many

---

[90] NATO, Group of Experts, *2020: Assured Security; Dynamic Engagement* (Brussels: NATO Press Office, 17 May 2010), http://www.nato.int/cps/en/natolive/official_texts_63654.htm (accessed July 10, 2010).NATO 2020: Assured Security; Dynamic Engagement, 5-8

[91] Ibid., 14-16

formal partnership arrangements and make recommendations for sustained engagement with the EU, UN, OSCE, Russia, potential future members, and several geostrategic regions. The purpose of this is to emphasize a comprehensive security approach that includes many potential partners.[92] The remainder of the report is spent addressing the difficult issues of funding reform, organization transformation, decision-making restructuring, and matching mission to available capability.[93] However, like earlier strategic concepts of the Alliance, their recommendations remain very broad and remain difficult to translate into an executable strategy that can then guide development of operational objectives expected to be fulfill by forces in the field.

Since the Group of Experts completed their report, the Secretary General Anders Fogh Rasmussen outlined NATO's priorities ahead of the November 2010 Summit of Heads of State and Government in Lisbon. Allies will have the chance to discuss the draft concept at a joint meeting of NATO Foreign and Defense Ministers prior to the summit. Discussions are expected to center on the Group's threat analysis and how best to respond to those threats, experiences in out-of-area operations, and the future of NATO partnership programs. The Secretary General also expects that the strategic concept will mandate a process of continual reform that ensures common funding and joint procurement.[94]

Above all, consensus among allies and the functioning of NATO's integrated military command has been pushed to its limits from the debate about national caveats and the strain on Alliance resources to support operations in Afghanistan. Therefore, the debate about the lessons to be learned from Afghanistan, and the future of similar operations, is bound to have an impact on the new Strategic Concept. Their report lists five distinct principles they recommend to be

---

[92] NATO, *2020: Assured Security; Dynamic Engagement*, 33-28

[93] Ibid., 31-45

[94] General Anders Fogh Rasmussen, "Secretary General previews preparations for Lisbon Summit", NATO Headquarters (Brussels: NATO Press Office, 15 Sep 2010), http://www.nato.int/cps/en/natolive/news_66221.htm (accessed November 4, 2010)

featured in the new Strategic Concept to set conditions for success in Afghanistan: Alliance

cohesion, unified command, effective planning and public diplomacy, a comprehensive

civilian/military approach, and the need to deploy forces at a strategic distance for an extended

period of time.[95] Interestingly the Group of Experts stated very explicitly that NATO is a regional

organization and that the new Strategic Concept should prescribe guidelines for the Alliance to

use to determine when and where to apply its limited resources outside Alliance borders.[96]

---

[95] NATO, *2020: Assured Security; Dynamic Engagement*, 9.

[96] They recommend eight guidelines that are intended to drive the NAC decision-making process: imminence of threat to allies, ineffectiveness of other options, willingness to provide capabilities, timeliness of response, collateral impact on other operations, domestic and international support, conformity to international law and consequence of inaction. NATO, *2020: Assured Security; Dynamic Engagement*, 33.

A Strategy for the Next Decade

Conclusions

NATO has agreed on the importance of combating terrorism and has subsequently tied its response to a success in Afghanistan. In order for NATO to fulfill its role in the ISAF and strengthen the fragile Afghanistan state, there must be consensus and ample political will among NATO allies to continue to prioritize Afghanistan. If the Alliance succeeds in Afghanistan, it will demonstrate its continued international relevance with its out-of-area operations and establish a legitimate precedent for joint European and American action against a shared common threat outside of its territorial boundaries. However, as warned by then Secretary General Jaap de Hoop Scheffer, failure could mean the decline of the Alliance, in both unity and strategic scope. [97] A failure of this nature would demonstrate the divisive nature of terrorism as a threat.

Since operations in Afghanistan transitioned to NATO control, regular negotiating with allies regarding burden sharing has been required. The force levels of participating countries have varied dramatically, as did the division of labor in both quantity and type. [98] The multilayered command structure continues to present challenges. While many of these complexities changed over the course of the operations, they demonstrate the difficulties in transitioning a peacetime alliance structure to an effective wartime footing. Further complicating matters, the issue of caveats has plagued the ISAF, with between 50–80 known caveats limiting NATO commanders during the course of operations in Afghanistan. Yet, with the current decision-making bureaucracy of the Alliance, these caveats are the only way that member nations can contribute to operations, while still appeasing governments and populations back home. This profoundly

---

[97] BBC News, "Nato 'can't allow Afghan failure'," *BBC News*, February 19, 2009. http://news.bbc.co.uk/go/pr/fr/-/2/hi/south_asia/7900367.stm (accessed November 17, 2010);

[98] P. A. Weitsman, "With a Little Help from our Friends? The Costs of Coalition Warfare," *Origins: Current Events in Historical Perspective* 3, no. 1 (2009): http://ehistory.osu.edu/osu/origins/article.cfm?articleid=22.

affects operational flexibility and heightens burden-sharing problems. In other words, some countries' troops occupy space on the ground and provide international legitimacy but make little difference operationally.[99] The difficulties the alliance has encountered in Afghanistan, however, are precisely those it might encounter in making out-of-area operations a major future focus in its pending strategic concept.

The differences in strategic vision between member nations based on varying national interests and perceptions of threat make the task of identifying a coherent strategy for the alliance extremely challenging. Since the 1990s, the implied bargain critical to the strategic concept has been continued U.S. military engagement with Europe in exchange for allied support to out of area operations.[100] After six years of dithering NATO engagement in Afghanistan, this bargain looks increasingly one sided from a U.S. perspective, in terms of troops and funding. The problem is all the more acute given the fact that many NATO allies fighting in Afghanistan are doing so at significant domestic political cost and, in contrast with observers in the United States, view their contributions as not only significant but as complete commitment, especially considering total NATO troop contributions have exceeded and currently nearly match the US. The ongoing strategy review process offers an opportunity to build consensus within the alliance about the main threats it faces and how to counter them. As the global economic crisis increases pressure on allied defense budgets, it will become difficult to meet proportionate commitments from allies to sustain their military forces. This challenging process will ultimately require skilled, allied political leadership advised by creative, problem-focused military leadership.

---

[99] David P. Auerswald and Stephen M. Saideman, "NATO at War: Understanding the Challenges of Caveats in Afghanistan" (paper presented at the Annual Meeting of the American Political Science Association, Toronto, CA, September 2-5th, 2009), http://www.aco nato.int/resources/1/documents/NATO%20at%20War.pdf.

[100] Michael Ruehle, "Changing Policy or Staying the Course," *World Security Network*, June 11, 2007, http://www.worldsecuritynetwork.com/showArticle3.cfm?article_id=14497 (accessed October 10, 2010

Military alliances can be difficult to manage during peacetime, let alone during times of external conflict. Consensus decision-making structures that foster cohesion and unanimity during peacetime do not readily transfer to wartime operations, when timely and concise action is required. The institutionalization of procedures that enhance transparency and facilitate cooperation in peacetime, as has occurred in NATO, may undermine fighting effectiveness during wartime. Furthermore, as both Kosovo and Afghanistan have demonstrated, NATO continues to suffer from significant interoperability issues. Kosovo and Afghanistan offer evidence that the Alliance's decision-making apparatus impinges on operational flexibility and organizational cohesion. Above all, it is clear that the choice of strategy formulation matters compellingly in war-fighting effectiveness.

Recommendations

The observations here bear on the nature of multilateralism and the design of alliances. Wartime alliances struggle with cohesion. Cohesion is fostered and maintained during wartime by clear objectives, threats that are perceived similarly by member states, and when attention is paid to cultural differences. Even in the absence of a unified chain of command, effective staff integration is manifest. The demands on such an institutional structure are significant and likely create more difficulties in implementing plans for war. While in the Kosovo case these conflicts did not frustrate NATO's ability to achieve its goals, the path toward achieving them was difficult, beginning with establishing those goals. This difficulty has been magnified in Afghanistan by the even greater convoluted command structure, national caveats, operational challenges and merely the distance, in both time and space, at which NATO is operating.[101]

---

[101] Michael Ruehle, "Changing Policy or Staying the Course," *World Security Network*, June 11, 2007, http://www.worldsecuritynetwork.com/showArticle3.cfm?article_id=14497 (accessed October 10, 2010

The implications here are that NATO is a highly useful alliance with great utility during peacetime because of its focus on diplomacy. During wartime, more flexible and adaptable institutional structures are necessary for effective war prosecution with an emphasis on operational effectiveness.[102] The policy implications are straightforward. Retaining the Alliance and deepening the commitment to it in peacetime is crucial to being prepared when it is called into service. Yet, when caveats and excessively cautious rules of engagement prevent effective member participation, the Alliance must assess the consequences on operational flexibility before the operation commences. Above all, taking a closer look at the strategy of relying on a multilateral war fighting capability to guarantee collective security and address the threat at hand as is being done for Strategic Concept 2010 makes sense. Developing benchmarks to determine whether drastically reshaping Alliance strategy is necessary since absolute assertions regarding when the Alliance should be used in warfare cannot be made.

There is evidence indicating that NATO's strategic concept will continue to transform, and thus that NATO will continue to exist into the foreseeable future. As Secretary General Rasmussen most recently said in a speech hosted by the General Marshall Fund to debut the new Strategic Concept, "a lot must change in the way NATO does business."[103] He outlined three areas that the new concept will move to change the alliance. The first part, as has been a major part of each previous strategy, deals with modernization of NATO capabilities, which includes missile defense and cyberspace. The second recommendation deals with the dialogue that occurs between civilian and military planners, making them more complimentary, cooperative, and working in a coordinated fashion towards common aims. Although he did not identify specific

---

[102] Todd Sandler and Keith Hartley, *The Political Economy of NATO: Past, Present and into the 21st Century*, First Trade Paperback ed. (Cambridge, U.K.: Cambridge University Press, 1999), 232-234

[103] General Anders Fogh Rasmussen, "The New Strategic Concept: Active Engagement, Modern Defence" (lecture presented at the Transatlantic Centre of the German Marshall Fund, Brussels, Belgium, October 8, 2010), http://www.nato.int/cps/en/natolive/opinions_66727.htm (accessed November 3, 2010).

structural or procedural changes to affect this, he did specify that a comprehensive approach was most crucial in crisis management situations. Lastly, he hinted toward greater NATO engagement globally, through deeper and wider engagement with countries in order to foster cooperative security. It seems that this new concept will not be a great departure from those in the past, in that it will maintain common defense and political consultation as key pillars of the Alliance. However, it will not advocate a withdrawal of NATO from the global security scene and this seems to strongly promote the importance of the trans-Atlantic relationship in facing security issues in the future.

To address the challenges NATO faces outlined by the Secretary General the new strategic concept must first continue to foster consensus, which implies somewhat vague language, but at the same time, it must be prescriptive enough to outline a way forward toward improvement of the Alliance. Most relevant to this study is his proposal for increased dialogue between civilian and military planners, especially for crisis management situations. Nevertheless, without serious consideration of changes to the structural or procedural construct of the Alliance, the same challenges that the Alliance faced in Kosovo and Afghanistan will likely continue. One possible alternative for adjusting the decision-making bureaucracy in the Alliance would be to permit member nations to abstain from participation in out-of-area operations, while still permitting an interior coalition to operate under a NATO endorsement and have access to NATO capabilities. This change would permit the Alliance to continue to maintain a global legitimacy through internationally authorized out-of-area operations, while alleviating the requirement for national caveats in order to secure participation. Due to changes in the security environment, and despite the problems the Alliance has faced in Kosovo and Afghanistan, it is difficult to make any compelling argument that it should return to a more traditional common security mindset.

BIBLIOGRAPHY

Auerswald, David P. and Stephen M. Saideman, "NATO at War: Understanding the Challenges of Caveats in Afghanistan", (paper presented at the Annual Meeting of the American Political Science Association, Toronto, CA, September 2-5th, 2009), http://www.aco.nato.int/resources/1/documents/NATO%20at%20War.pdf.

Barno, David W., "Fighting 'the Other War': Counterinsurgency Strategy in Afghanistan, 2003-2005," *Military Review*, September/October 2007.

Basevich, Andrew J., and Eliot A. Cohen, eds. *War Over Kosovo*. Edited by Andrew J. Bacevich and Eliot A. Cohen. New York: Columbia University Press, 2002.

Bebler, Anton A. *The Challenge of NATO Enlargement*. Westport, Conn.: Praeger, 1999.

Burgess, Lisa "War in Afghanistan Has Improved Nato Forces, Official Says," *Stars and Stripes*, September 15, 2006. http://www.stripes.com/news/war-in-afghanistan-has-improved-nato-forces-official-says-1.54141 (accessed November 12, 2010).

Cohen, Eliot. *Supreme Command: Soldiers, Statesmen, and Leadership in Wartime*. First Edition ed. New York: Free Press, 2002.

Chivvis, Christopher S. *Recasting NATO's Strategic Concept: Possible Directions for the United States (Occasional Paper)*. Santa Monica, CA.: RAND Corporation, 2010.

Clark, Wesley K., *Waging Modern War:Bosnia, Kosovo, and the Future of Combat*. New York, NY: PublicAffairs, 2001.

Clausewitz, Carl von. *On War*. Edited by Michael Howard and Peter Paret. Princeton: Princeton University Press, 1989.

Daalder, Ivo H., and Michael E. O'Hanlon. *Winning Ugly: Nato's War to Save Kosovo*. Washington, D.C.: Brookings Institution Press, 2001.

Douglas, Frank R. *The United States, NATO, and a New Multilateral Relationship (PSI Reports)*. Westport, Conn.: Praeger, 2007.

Dannreuther, Roland, and John Peterson, *Security Strategies and Transatlantic Relations*. New York, NY: Routledge, 2006.

Government Accounting Office, "Kosovo Air Operations: Need to Maintain Alliance Cohesion Resulted in Doctrinal Departures," GAO-01-784, Washington: GAO, 2001.

Farrella, Theo. "Improving in War: Military Adaptation and the British in Helmand Province, Afghanistan, 2006-2009." *Journal of Strategic Studies*. 33, no. 4 (August 2010): 567-94. http://pdfserve.informaworld.com/896024_926058792.pdf (accessed November 14, 2010).

Hart B. H., Liddell, *Strategy*. New York: Signet, 1974.

Hendrickson, Ryan C. *Diplomacy and War at NATO: The Secretary General and Military Action after the Cold War*. Columbia, Mo.: University of Missouri, 2006.

Hope, Ian. "Unity of Command in Afghanistan: A Foresaken Principle of War." *Strategic Studies Institute* (November 2008): 7. http://www.StrategicStudiesInstitute.army.mil/ (accessed August 20, 2010).

Huntington, Samuel, *The Soldier and the State: The Theory of Politics of Civil-Military Relations*. Cambridge, MA: Belknap Press, 1983.

Janowitz, Morris., *The Professional Soldier: A Social and Political Portrait*. New York: Free Press, 1971.

Jordan, Robert S., *Political leadership in NATO: A study in multinational diplomacy (Westview special studies in international relations)*. Boulder, Colo.: Westview Press, 1979.

Kaplan, Lawrence S., *NATO 1948: The Birth of the Transatlantic Alliance*. Lanham, Md.: Rowman & Littlefield Publishers, Inc., 2007.

_____*The United States and NATO: The Formative Years*. Lexington, Ky.: Univ Pr of Kentucky, 1984.

Lambeth, Benjamin S., *NATO's Air War for Kosovo: A Strategic and Operational* Assessment, Washington: RAND, 2001.

Maloney, Sean M., *Enduring the Freedom: A Rogue Historian in Afghanistan*. Washington, DC.: Potomac Books Inc., 2005.

Mearsheimer, John J., *The Tragedy of Great Power Politics*. New York: W. W. Norton & Company, 2001.

Medcalf, Jennifer, *Going Global or Going Nowhere?: Nato's Role in Contemporary International Security*. New York: Peter Lang, 2008.

Menon, Rajan. *The End of Alliances*. New York, NY: Oxford University Press, 2008.

Moore, Rebecca R.. *NATO's New Mission: Projecting Stability in a Post-Cold War World*. Westport, CT: Praeger Security International General Interest-Cloth, 2007.

Morelli,Vincent, "NATO in Afghanistan: A Test of the Transatlantic Alliance," Congressional Research Service, October 23, 2008, 2.

NATO, North Atlantic Council, "Strasbourg / Kehl Summit Declaration." Strasbourg, France, (Brussels: NATO Press Office, 2009). http://www.nato.int/cps/en/natolive/news_52837.htm (accessed November 4, 2010)

_____*NATO Handbook*. Brussels: NATO Office of Information Belgium, 2001.

_____NATO Headquarters, "A Roadmap for the New Strategic Concept." NATO's New Strategic Concept. http://www.nato.int/strategic-concept/roadmap-strategic-concept.html#guiding (accessed July 10, 2010).

_____North Atlantic Council, "The Istanbul Declaration - Our security in a new era," Istanbul, Turkey, (Brussels: NATO Press Office, 28 June 2004), http://www.nato.int/cps/en/natolive/news_52837.htm (accessed November 4, 2010)

_____Cook, Frank, NATO Parliamentary Assembly, "Afghanistan: Assessing Progress and Key Challenges for the Alliance," (Brussels: NATO Press Office, 28 June 2007), http://www.nato-pa.int/default.Asp?SHORTCUT=1166 (accessed October 10, 2010)

_____Founding Act on Mutual Relations, Cooperation and Security between NATO and the Russian Federation signed in Paris, France, May 27, 1997, http://www.nato.int/cps/en/natolive/official_texts_25468.htm (accessed November 14, 2010)

_____Group of Experts, chaired by Madeleine K. Albright, *2020: Assured Security; Dynamic Engagement*, (Brussels: NATO Press Office, 17 May 2010), http://www.nato.int/cps/en/natolive/official_texts_63654.htm (accessed July 10, 2010).

_____Pedlow, Gregory, ed. *Nato Strategy Documents 1949-1969*. Brussels, Belgium: NATO Information Service, 1997. http://www.nato.int/docu/stratdoc/eng/intro.pdf (accessed September 21, 2010).

Naylor, Sean. *Not a Good Day to Die: The Untold Story of Operation Anaconda*. 1St Edition ed. New York: Berkley Hardcover, 2005.

Obama, Barack, "The Way Forward in Afghanistan and Pakistan" (lecture presented at the Remarks by the President in Address to the Nation, West Point, NY, December 1, 2009), http://www.whitehouse.gov/the-press-office/remarks-president-address-nation-way-forward-afghanistan-and-pakistan (accessed November 20, 2010).

Pressman, Jeremy. *Warring friends: Alliance Restraint in International Politics*. Ithaca, NY: Cornell University Press, 2008.

Rasmussen, Anders Fogh. "The New Strategic Concept: Active Engagement, Modern Defence." Lecture, Transatlantic Centre of the German Marshall Fund, Brussels, Belgium, October 8, 2010. http://www.nato.int/cps/en/natolive/opinions_66727.htm (accessed November 3, 2010).

Rohde, David and David E. Sanger, "How a 'Good War' in Afghanistan Went Bad," *New York Times*, August 12, 2007. http://www.nytimes.com/2007/08/12/world/asia/12afghan.html?pagewanted=all (accessed November 18, 2010).

Ruehle, Michael, "Changing Policy or Staying the Course," *World Security Network*, June 11, 2007. http://www.worldsecuritynetwork.com/showArticle3.cfm?article_id=14497 (accessed October 10, 2010)

Rupp, Richard. *NATO after 9/11: An Alliance in Continuing Decline*. New York: Palgrave Macmillan, 2006.

Sandler, Todd, Keith Hartley, and Arthur Wells. *The Political Economy of NATO: Past, Present and into the 21st Century*. Cambridge, UK: Cambridge Univ Pr, 2000.

Schmitt, Eric "Obama Issues Order for More Troops in Afghanistan," *New York Times*, November 30, 2009. http://www.nytimes.com/2009/12/01/world/asia/01orders.html (accessed October 10, 2010).

Sloan, Stanley. *NATO, the European Union, and the Atlantic community: the Transatlantic Bargain Challenged*. Lanham, MD: Rowman & Littlefield Pub Inc, 2005.

Snyder, Glenn. *Alliance Politics*. Ithaca, NY: Cornell University Press, 2007.

Solomon, Gerald B. *The NATO Enlargement Debate, 1990-1997: The Blessings of Liberty (The Washington Papers)*. Westport, Conn.: Praeger, 1998.

Stuart, Douglas, and William T. Tow. *The Limits of Alliance: NATO Out-of-Area Problems since 1949 (Perspectives on Security)*. Baltimore: The Johns Hopkins University Press, 1990.

Thies, Wallace. *Friendly rivals: Bargaining and Burden Shifting in NATO*. Armonk, NY: M.E. Sharpe, 2002.

Walt, Stephen M. *The Origins of Alliances,* Ithaca: Cornell University Press, 1990.

Wijk, Rob De. *NATO on the Brink of the New Millennium: The Battle for Consensus*. 1st English ed. London: Brassey's UK, 1997.

Yost, David S. *NATO Transformed: The Alliances New Roles in International Security*. Washington D.C.: United States Institute of Peace, 1999.

_____ "NATO's 1999 Stratigic Concept" in *Security Strategies: NATO, the United States and the European Union.* Rome, IT: NATO Defense College, 2005

www.ingramcontent.com/pod-product-compliance
Lightning Source LLC
Chambersburg PA
CBHW080611290526
45790CB00007B/2723